Me and My Shadows

Shadow Puppet Fun for

Kids of All Ages

Enhanced with Practical Paper pastimes

Bud Banis, Ph.D.

with Puppets by Elizabeth Adams

Copyright

Me and My Shadows Shadow Puppet Fun for Kids of All Ages Enhanced with Practical Paper Pastimes. This edition is expanded and amended from previous editions.
Paperback 7.5x9.25, 120 pp.

CreateSpace Independent Publishing Platform

LCCN: 2013902201

Some Shadow characters and descriptions were refurbished and updated from *Shadow Pictures My Children Love to Make* by Elizabeth Adams, published in 1910 by Lloyd Adams Noble. Cover graphic—by Bud Banis, Ph.D., inspired in part by the concept from Elizabeth Adams.
Some of the shadow puppets in this book were included in Me and *My Shadows : shadow puppet fun for kids of all ages /* puppets by Elizabeth Adams ; revised by Dr. Bud Banis, (ISBN 1-888725- 44-3) BeachHouse Books (2000)

for
Kate & Julia

Table of Contents

Me and My Shadows

A Book Planned to Entertain Children of All Ages

Entertainment doesn't always have to be expensive or require elaborate equipment. Years ago, many thought shadow-pictures were possible only on stages where accommodations could be made for special lighting systems. This may be true for large audiences and startling effects, but shadow puppets are now among the simplest toys and tools for amusement. Lights strong enough are to be found everywhere, and the basic equipment is always at your fingertips, so to speak, or "right at hand."

Each night when you turn on your lights, you must realize that your shadow is cast behind you on the wall. Now if, instead of standing your whole body before the light, you merely hold your hand there, you will find that you have formed a shadow-picture of your hand. And if your wall paper is not a dark shade you will discover that this shadow-picture, which you make of your hand by the aid of your home light, is equally as pleasing as the shadows made by a more intense light — though, perhaps, it may not be as clearly defined. If you want to increase the "sharpness" of this shadow, you can simply stretch an ordinary sheet across the wall so that there is a marked contrast between the black shadow and the white background. An easy way is to throw a sheet over the top of the door and make your pictures on that. Any flat surface will prove satisfactory, providing, of course, your light is shining directly upon it. Generally speaking, the stronger the light and the whiter the "screen," the better the shadow picture will be!

It doesn't matter what kind of light you use, as long as you can focus it on just one part of the wall. The rest of the room should then be darkened as much as possible. Never use two lights side by side, for then each would cast a shadow and give you a doubled picture. Always have your light strong enough to cast a sharp shadow of your hands; or, if your light is weak, bring the light close enough to your hands so that the shadow is distinct.

The exact distance to hold your hands from the light in order to cast a sharp shadow can only be determined by experiment. The nearer the light you place your hand the larger will be the shadow; but the nearer the hand is held to the wall, the more distinct the shadow will be.

Forming these pictures is relatively simple. The illustrations in this book have all been specially drawn from the particular poses of children's hands. It might be difficult at first to hold your fingers in all the positions. These are probably good exercises for improving dexterity and finger control! I hope you will find each illustration self-explanatory. The poses shown here are all pretty easy, and with a little practice, can be mastered by anyone.

Shadow pictures are always available, don't cost anything, and will provide endless rainy afternoon or after dinner delight.

Part I
Shadow Puppets and How
to Make Them

Suggestions:

Don't forget that the sleeve must be folded back so that the bare arm casts a gracefully bending shadow which will form the swan's neck By lowering and raising the little finger of the right hand and at the same time straightening the wrist a little, it will seem as if the bird is eating. If the left hand is moved backward and forward the swan will appear to flap her wings. By moving both arms forward, the shadow will seem to "swim" away, fading from sight as the arms pass from their position before the light.

The Swan

Suggestions:

By lowering and raising your little fingers you can make the birds open and close their bills. If you tightly hold the first and second fingers of each hand with the thumb, then raise them just enough to let the light pass through, each of the swans will then have an eye. You must be careful to keep the back of your right hand well away from the light, or the bird's head will be too fat.

Two Ducks in line

Suggestions:

Moving your fingers in this pattern may take some practice. If it is too difficult for the fingers to hold their positions, let your little finger make the lower part of the bird's bill, and then bend your ring finger behind the second finger. To make the birds open and close their eyes, do not lower your first finger which is bent, but move your thumb back and forth to cover the opening between the first and second finger. If you let the swans peck at each other, keep your wrists stiff so that your hands will not turn and change the whole shadow-picture.

Two Ducks Talking

Suggestions:

When you cross your thumbs in making the bird's head, be sure to keep the left directly above the right, For if the thumbs press straight against each other the light will then strike them both; and they will cast a shadow which will make it appear as if the bird has two heads. Keep the palms of your hands always opened towards the light. If you wave your hands, it will seem as if the bird is flying. Do not let your fingers bend so that the light can pass between them or the bird will look split down the middle. That would look silly!

Flying Bird

Suggestions:

In fixing your hands to make the shadow-picture of an eagle's head, bend the little finger of your left hand far enough down so that it will not cover the opening formed by the other fingers and spoil the bird's eye. Keep the fingers of your right hand together so that the light can strike only the index finger, and the line which shapes the upper part of the eagle's beak will not be wider than the lower. The left arm should always be held so close to the right that the light cannot shine between them.

Eagle Head

Suggestions:

Keep your back to the light and raise your right arm until it is level with your shoulder. The outline of the cat's body is best made by wrapping a shawl—or even a napkin—around the right arm. The ends of this shawl can then be held in place by the left hand which should grip the elbow of the right arm. Do not let the left hand come below the right elbow, or it will cast a shadow. Extend the index finger of the left hand just enough so that it will form the cat's tail.

Cat with Tail

Suggestions:

Keep the little finger of your right hand bent tightly against your palm, but hold the other fingers loose—just as they are drawn. It will then be easy to make the mouth of the shadow-picture dog. Now, if you should want to force your dog to "howl," move your right hand by bending it upward from the wrist with a jerk, and at the same time lower your thumb. When you finally fix your left hand in the proper position for the picture, do not move it to make the dog close his eye — simply lower your little finger.

Puppy Head

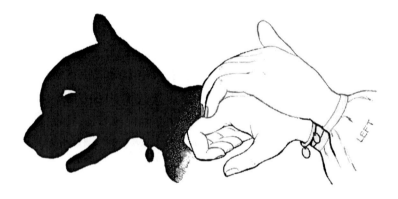

Suggestions:

If you can't hold your fingers in the way that they are drawn, change the position of your right hand. Bend all the fingers, except the thumb and little finger, against the palm. Turn your right hand over and, bending the left thumb to the palm, place your right thumb in the position which the left formerly held. The bull's horns will then be made by the shadow of the thumb and little finger of the right hand. This picture can be made only when the light shines from the left, striking your hands from the side.

Bull Head

Suggestions:

The deer's nose is formed, as you see, by the first three fingers of the right hand. The best effect will be produced if these fingers are kept close together so that the light cannot strike each one and cast a shadow of three fingers. Touch the tip of the index finger to the tip of the ring finger, and then let the long second finger rest on the top of those two. Try to hold them all tight so that they will look like one big finger. You can do it. Keep the fingers that make the deer's horns straight!

Deer Head

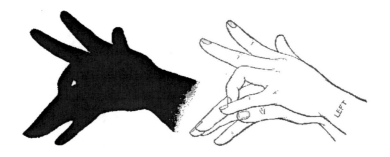

Suggestions:

Bend and straighten the fingers of the left hand, moving them in a lazy fashion to imitate the swinging of an elephant's trunk. Be sure to keep the fingers in a line behind the index finger so that the light will not strike them all and cast a broad shadow. Bending the fingers up until the tips touch the palm will make it seem as if the elephant is eating. If the thumb of the left hand does not reach out far enough, project your little finger. The elephant will then have longer tusks. Don't let the light shine between your wrists or the elephant will have a hole in his head!

Elephant

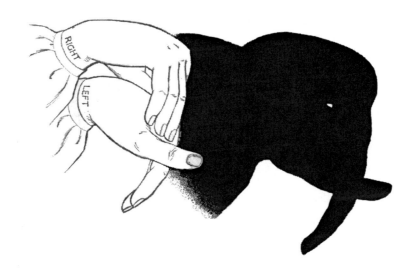

Suggestions:

The lower jaw of the horse is made by the shadow of the ring finger and the little finger of the right hand. These fingers should be held one behind the other. A handkerchief rolled up and tied around the wrists will cast the shadow of the horse's collar. To imitate the actions of a horse chewing his oats, move the fingers of the left hand slowly to make the "mouth" move. Bend your arms up and down at the elbow. This will cause the horse's head to sway in a life-like manner while he is "eating."

Horse with Collar

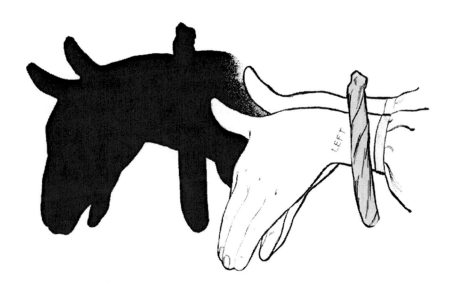

Suggestions:

The position of your head is important in this one, as the shadow of the top of your head makes the body of the duck. If you don't hold your left hand level with your shoulder, your head will cast a shadow in the wrong place. Hold the wrist of your right hand tightly against your forehead and don't use the left hand at all. The ring finger of the right hand should be held closely behind the long second finger or the light will strike them both and then the upper part of the bird's bill will be wider than the lower.

Duck Swimming

Suggestions:

An ordinary china plate should be held in the left hand to cast a shadow which will represent the shell of the snail. Keep your left hand in its fixed position and move your right arm so that the snail seems to draw back into his shell. Grip your right elbow with your left hand, then hold the plate between your thumb and elbow. The general effect is better when the shadow is made in this way. As you make the snail crawl forward, let him slowly move his horns back and forth. Do not bend your fingers!

Snail

Suggestions:

If you ever want to make a shadow-picture in the opposite direction from the drawings, just use your right hand where the left is marked, and the left where the right is marked. Compare the rabbit on the cover with the rabbit on this page! See how easy it is! By changing the positions of the shadow-pictures so that they face one another, you can have two or three little children all making pictures together with you. Let your rabbit shut his eye, move his front paws, and wave his ears.

Rabbit Body

Suggestions:

To make the picture of a wolf, the three fingers of the left hand which cast the shadow representing the nose must be held almost one behind the other—not one above the other. In this way the palm of the hand is held practically parallel with the floor. If you then just touch the tip of the index finger of your right hand to the middle joint of the long second finger of your left hand, the wolf's eye can easily be made. Stretch the thumb of the right hand forward and bend the index finger of the left hand backward.

Long-nosed Wolf

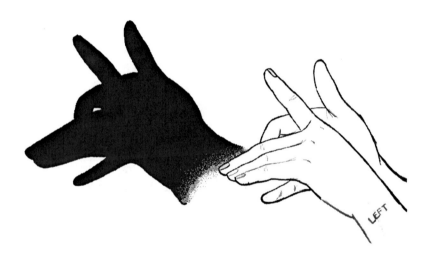

Suggestions:

If you have difficulty making the mouth of the shadow-picture goat, take away his beard. Let the little finger of the left hand form the goat's lower jaw. Hold the other three fingers close together to cast the shadow of his nose. In this way you can make an excellent shadow-picture without cramping your little finger. The first two fingers of the right hand should be stretched out very straight for they make the goat's horns—and remember not to bend them when you move your thumb to imitate the twitching of the goat's ear.

Goat

Suggestions:

Your hands take almost the same positions in making the shadow-picture of the rabbit's head that they did in making the goat's on the previous page. It is hard to form the animal's mouth. The fingers must be bent, for if they are stretched out, the rabbit will have a long lower jaw. The right hand will cover any opening which may be left between the thumb and the little finger. Move the right hand to the right so that the rabbit will close his eye, then bend the fingers so that he will seem to wave his ears.

Rabbit Head

Suggestions:

In making the shadow-picture of the donkey's head, the hardest part is setting the position of the index finger of the right hand. If you can make a good eye for your donkey, the rest of the picture will be simple. The fingers of both hands may be arranged in any way at all, if a sufficient space is left between them to represent the donkey's mouth. The fingers which form the nose and mouth should be kept tight together. Do not let the light shine on them in a way that you can recognize the shadow of a particular finger.

Donkey Head

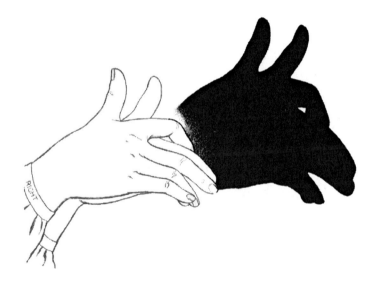

Suggestions:

Keep the long second finger of the right hand directly behind the index finger so that the nose in the picture will be an unbroken shadow of the two fingers. By raising the thumb of your right hand to touch the little finger of your left hand, you can make the lady close her eye. If you want to have it seem as if she is talking, make her lips move by raising the little finger and the ring finger. Don't bend the fingers that make the nose.

A "curmudgeon" is a grouchy old man.

Old Lady or Curmudgeon

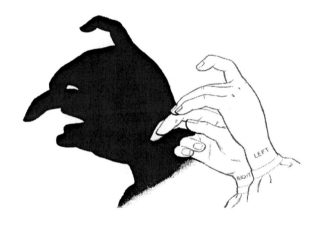

Suggestions:

When you open and close the mouths of your shadow-picture figures to make them seem as if they are talking, speak the words for them. If you have committed any little pieces to memory, let your shadow people "speak" them. If you make one figure, and then let someone make another to appear opposite yours, the two shadow-pictures will seem to be engaged in conversation. If you learn to fix your fingers so that the lips of the shadow-picture figures move naturally, it is great fun to hear the old man tell a story.

Old Man's Head with Cap

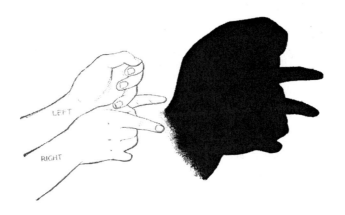

Suggestions:

Let the thumb of your left hand hold the two middle fingers of your right hand against the palm. In this way it is possible to keep all your fingers held closely in position. If your light is not very strong, the shadow will not be distinct, and in this picture it will be difficult to make the outlines sharp for the lady's mouth so you can make her talk. This one is hard to show in action, as it is too easy to move your hands a little and make a completely different shadow.

This character looks very much like Judy, of the Punch and Judy puppet team, well-known around the world in the early 1900's. Later, you will see how to represent both Punch and Judy, and you will be able to thrill and impress your parents and friends with your knowledge of Victorian-age entertainment!

Old Biddy (Judy)

Suggestions:

This one will take a little practice and will improve your finger control. It is not at all easy to make the mouth of the shadow-picture devil! To allow suitable space to represent the mouth, the tip of the ring finger and the tip of the long second finger must be pressed tightly against the palm. Try to keep your fingers from slipping out of place. The lower part of the right hand must be tilted away from the light. The little finger and the ring finger of the left hand may be either doubled up or stretched out across the back of your right hand.

The Devil!

Suggestions:

If your only difficulty in making the devil's image was keeping your little finger in place, this picture of the Indian should be easy. With the exception of the little finger, your right hand is in the same position as for a devil. By bending the index finger of the right hand, you will cause the Indian's nose to grow shorter. Move the fingers of your left hand so that the Indian will seem to shake his feathers. Raise the ring finger and little finger of the left hand and make him "shout" his war-cries.

Indian Chief

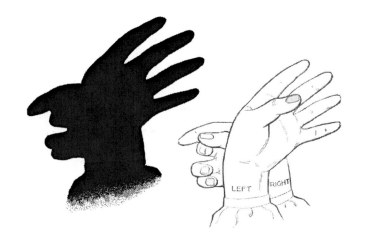

Suggestions:

In making the pictures of this book, it doesn't really matter whether the light strikes the front or the back of the hands if the fingers are arranged properly to cast the right shadow. You will observe that the right hand on this page is in exactly the same position as the left hand on the next page. As we saw at the beginning of the book, when we made the picture of the rabbit, all shadows can be reversed simply by using the right hand in place of the left, and the left for the right. Here we learn how to reverse the positions of the hand.

Knave with Feathered Hat

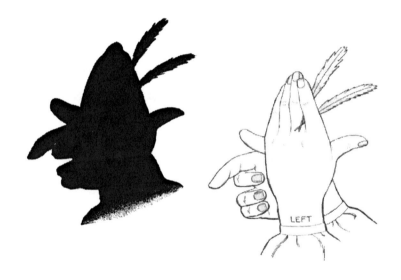

51

Suggestions:

You don't have to use both hands to make a shadow-picture. A cardboard can be cut in almost any shape to form a hat, then held in the left hand where the fingers will make the nose and the mouth. If you hold your right hand a little farther from the light than you are holding your left, a smaller shadow will be cast, and the character will have a hand of its own. You can make him scratch his nose, lift a glass to his lips, or use his hands in whatever way you wish!

Old Man with a Hat or a Witch?

Suggestions:

Again, both hands can be arranged exactly as they were for the last shadow-picture—and any other form of cardboard cut-out used. Here we have either an old man in his night cap, or perhaps a jester! Remember that the shadow will look more lifelike if you cut an "eye" in the cardboard. However, if you intend to use your right hand so that the man will move his hat in any way, it is better not to let him have an eye. If he has an eye, each time you move the cardboard hat the eye will move about also. That would be a little weird!

Jester

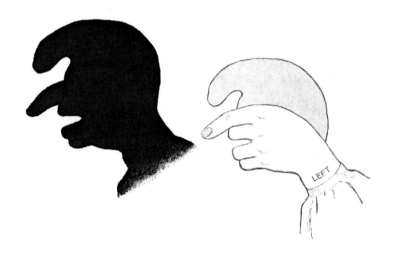

Suggestions:

The left hand is still in the same position as it was when the last shadow-picture was made, but here we have cut our piece of cardboard in the shape of a woman's head instead of a man's hat. You can make any kind of a shadow person you desire if you simply take your scissors and cut the cardboard in the proper shape. Let the lady here fan herself. While you are making her open and close her mouth, bend your forefinger just a little. This will cause the lady to move her nose and the effect is really funny.

Old Lady with a Fan

Suggestions:

A cardboard could be cut in the shape of a soldier's hat and held between the index finger and the thumb of the left hand. The expression on the soldier's face will depend entirely upon the positions of the four fingers of your right hand. By bringing the little finger closer to the palm you will take away his beard. By extending the index finger you will make his nose grow longer. By lowering the ring finger and the little finger you can cause the man's mouth to open.

Musketeer

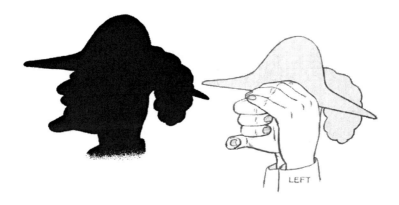

Suggestions:

This drawing shows what can be accomplished if you use the cardboard cut-outs in making shadow-pictures. The figure shows the result of making changes in the right hand position suggested in the previous, musketeer example.

See how very different the shadows are. If you would cut out enough cardboard hats you could make the shadows represent many different characters, and so act out a little play. The two shown look like the Punch and Judy show puppets that were discussed a few pages back. It would be easy to put on a very animated show using these two characters.

Punch & Judy

LEFT   RIGHT

Suggestions:

Does this picture seem strange? Why is that?

Since the right hand is held as near the light as the left, the man's hand is as large as his head! When you make a complete figure with one hand and then use the shadow which the other hand casts to represent the figure's hand, do not forget to keep that hand farther away from the light so that it will cast a smaller shadow.Be sure to make the hands of your shadow people smaller than their heads.

Scholar, Headmaster

Suggestions:

To make the horse's head narrow, keep your fingers flat in the light so the three fingers look more like one.

Move your left arm slowly up and down, bending it at the elbow, so that your horse will appear to be galloping. Jerk the right hand backward and make the jockey bring the horse to a walk. When the jockey is moving, keep the ring finger and the little finger of the right hand close behind the long second finger.

Horse Race with Jockey

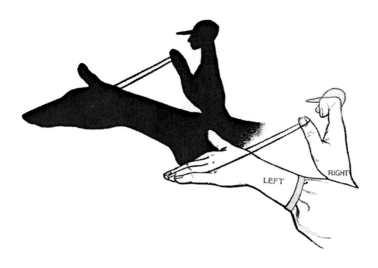

Suggestions:

Instead of holding the cardboard boat in your left hand, you can stand it on top of a book at the edge of a table. The book will cast a shadow which can represent the water with the fish at the end of the line behind the book so it doesn't cast a shadow. Your fisherman can then be seen patiently waiting for a bite. You can jerk the line a little with your left hand from behind the book. Then let the fisherman, after struggling hard, pull the little fish up triumphantly and drop him in the boat.

Fisherman in Boat

Part II
Practical Paper Pastimes

Practical paper pastimes

These projects, some classical, some fairly new, were chosen for simplicity — for quick and easy entertainment:

- ➢ Need a water cup in a hurry?
- ➢ Want to play ventriloquist with a folded paper hand puppet?
- ➢ Want to see water climb up a paper towel and understand how trees get water from the ground up to the leaves?
- ➢ Can you remember how to make that newspaper hat you made when you were a kid? Or the classical paper boat?
- ➢ Know how to quickly make simple animated cartoons with a sheet of paper and a pencil?
- ➢ Did you ever write secret messages on a rubber band?

This new expanded version of *Me and My Shadows* has been enhanced by adding practical paper projects derived from various sources.

A simple folded paper cup

How many times have you been out someplace and wished for a more convenient way to take a drink of water from a drinking fountain?

Most people have probably seen this simple paper cup you can make in a hurry from just a sheet of paper. But most people probably don't think of this or remember it when an opportunity arises to use this simple tool.

All you need is a sheet of paper folded as shown in the photos:

first fold the sheet down the center, longways. then fold in the tabs as shown.

 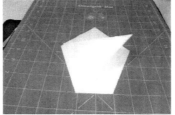

Fold down the front top flap.

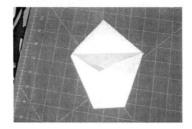

Then turn it over and fold down the other top flap on the other side.

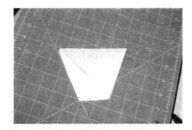

We fold over the top to stiffen it, and open it to hold the liquid. Open up the cup at the open end.

Here are a few other views

As long as the paper isn't porous it can be used numerous times before it deteriorates.

If the paper is porous, such as a paper towel, then your cup becomes a filter. This can be useful to remove solids such as coffee grounds that accidentally came through your coffee maker. Tear off a corner, and it's a funnel! Make it big enough, and it's a hat!

(Of course, with me, as well as most guys, almost everything gets tried out as a hat at some point!)

Simple quick puppet from a small paper bag:

Hardly any need to give instructions on this. The pictures are worth more than the words!

All you need is a small paper bag, suitable for the puppeteer's hand size, and a few marking pens. I'm sure your art work would be more impressive than mine!

Add a dash of imagination and a little ventriliquist's skills and you have a friend for life!

Folded Paper Hand Puppet.

This ventriloquist puppet is on of my favorites.

It's easier to work than the paper bag puppet, so it's worth the extra complexity to put together.

If you are showing this to a younger child, it can raise suspense to watch the sequential folds and wonder what the eventual product will be.

Start with a square piece of paper. fold one corner of a regular letter-size sheet to give you a guide, then You can easily trim off a strip to make it into a square. Save the trimming. We can use it later to make cartoon movies!

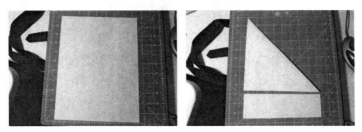

Take your triangle and fold the two corners on the enclosed side to make a smaller triangle.

Open it up, then use the folds as a guide to fold the corners into the center to give a smaller square.

Turn it over and fold the new corners in to give an even smaller square. When you turn this over yet again, you'll see that each corner now has a flap that can be pulled up to give space for your fingers.

Now, turn it over again, and note that there are flaps at each corner.

It can be a little easier to get everything folded in the right way if you fold the square in half so the finger flaps are to the outside. you can do this folding both vertically and horizontally to get the puppet pliable.

Insert your fingers under the corner flaps and look at the front side. Draw a face on the puppet and it will look a little more recognizable as a puppet face.

Use a marker to paint in some eyes, and a suggestion of lips.

Ah! at last we get to play!

You can demonstrate your ventriloquist dummy as you did with the paper bag puppet. Speak normally to the puppet, then speak for the puppet (trying not to move your lips when the puppet is speaking, to maintain the illusion that the puppet is responding to you.) With very little practice, you can become quite adept at carrying on conversations with your dummy.

I've had a lot of fun over the years with this particular puppet. There were a few notable funny experiences when I was showing my folded paper masterpiece to children:

One time my grandson happened to be eating out of a bowl of popcorn when we made the puppet. So, of course, the puppet had to have some popcorn.

My grandson, Clayton, took the puppet, dug into the popcorn bowl, and then, of course, it seemed logical to pretend that the puppet regurgitated the popcorn back into the bowl! This was accompanied by making appropriate gross sounds!

I urged him to demonstrate this new skill to his mother.

Her comment was, "I'm so proud!"

Another time I was showing this puppet to my nephew, Richard, who was about two years old at the time.

When I demonstrated my skills as a ventriloquist, Richard took action against the intruder and hit it with a wooden spoon!

That smarted!

My sister, Anne, laughed.

Today, Richard is grown up and has his own son, Ren. I wonder if he still has the wooden spoon.

A Magic Paper Towel Siphoning System

Did you ever wonder how a plant gets water and dissolved nutrients from the soil up to its leaves? The water has to flow uphill against gravity!

The mechanism for this marvel is called **"capillary action."** Water and other liquids will defy gravity and climb up a porous material. The reason for this is that water molecules tend to stick together and also have an attraction for the porous surface that's provided for in the climb. So inside the bark of a tree or bush, water can travel by this natural phenomenon, ultimately reaching the highest leaves in the biggest tree.

The water brings with it minerals from the soil and other nutrients that the leaves can use to actually manufacture new leaves, new branches, and more wood. The process involves combining carbon dioxide from the air using the energy of sunlight in a process called **"photosynthesis."** ("making something new by using the energy of light").

This wonderful process recycles the **carbon dioxide** that is exhaled by animals and produced by burning wood, coal or petroleum used for heat or energy.

In this way, nature has a biological/chemical cycle to provide us with fuel, vegetables for food, materials to build new houses.

You can demonstrate this marvelous process using just a few glasses, a little water, and a paper towel. Fill one of the glasses partway with water, and leave the other glass empty. Crumple the paper towel so that it can be used as a pathway between the two glasses, and put one end in each class. To make this a little more visible I put some food coloring into the water in the glass.

Watch what happens. Pretty quickly the water from the full cup will start to rise up the paper towel, wetting the paper towel as it spreads out and moves against gravity. After a while the water will reach the top of the paper towel between the glasses and start to descend into the empty glass.

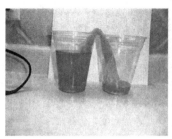 

You have to be patient with this, perhaps leave it all day or overnight.

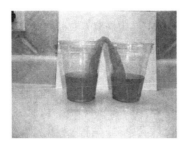

After some period of time the water in both glasses will be at the same level. At this point water molecules should be moving both ways in the paper towel but it will have reached an **equilibrium** so that both glasses have the same level of water in them.

After a while when the level in the glasses had equaled out, I took one glass and raised it up a little, then left it for a little while longer.

As you can see from the pictures, the levels in the two glasses reached a new equilibrium, such that the water was at the same absolute height in the glasses, with less water in a glass that was higher.

There is a saying, "water seeks its own level."

Think of other experiments you could do with this system. Install your paper towel siphoning system and observe what happens.

Folded Paper Boats

This is a classic. When I was a kid, we often made paper party hats and other toys out of folded newspaper.

A lot of newspapers have decreased the size of the paper to save money, but some news sheets may be large enough to make a hat that can even fit an adult-size head.

You can make these same toys in a more manageable size from ordinary letter-size paper. To make the classical sailboat That you might have seen in an illustrated copy of the fairy tale, *The Steadfast Tin Soldier*, by Hans Christian Anderson, start with a letter size paper. fold it in half the long way, then fold it in half again the other way. opening up just the second fold, you can use the crease as a guide for the centerline.

fold the top two corners into the centerline, then fold the top sheet of the bottom segment up.

 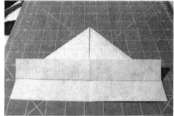

Turn the paper over and fold the bottom segment of the other side up, towards you, so the bottom segments are folded up on opposite sides of the paper.

Open up the cone, folding it in the other direction to give a rhombus, a diamond-shape figure. You will have to tuck the ends of the folded bottom segments together to get it to lie flat in this configuration.

Now, fold the bottom corners up on their respective sides to give a small triangle shape.

At this point, you could just open it up on the open side to make a a small hat.

Roll it a little and fold the open "hat" into a yet smaller **rhombus**, (diamond-shape). Then repeat the process of folding up the corners on the respective sides to give an even *smaller* triangle.

Allow this last set of folds to open so that the project can sit flat on the surface.

Pulling out gently on the corners at the top of the "sail" makes this a little more recognizable as a play sailboat.

Reshaping your creation carefully will give you a toy "sailboat" that can actually be floated on water.

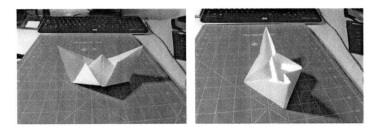

Or actually float it in a sink of water. You way have to manipulate the edges a bit so water doesn't come into the boat.

Imagine a tin soldier floating in the boat.

The "Boat" Can Also be a Hat

Of course, at any stage during this process, the project can be opened into "hats" of various shapes and sizes

To make a larger hat that you can actually wear, start with a bigger piece of paper.

The more folds you make and the more layers of paper involved, the sturdier the hat. I wouldn't try to use it as a safety helmet, however.

A More Complex Box-Shaped Hat

The next project has actually served a practical purpose for adults--painters and newspaper printers, as a quick disposable hat to protect their heads from paint and ink. When the day's work was done, the paper hat could simply be thrown away and he could make a new one for tomorrow.

Thus, this paper hat is commonly known as a "newsman's hat" or a "painter's hat."

This box-shaped hat is a lot more complicated to make, but if you start with a large enough piece of newspaper, it can be quite comfortable and serviceable.

The project starts almost like the boat/hat project.

Starting with a double sheet of newspaper, fold the closed corners into the centerline as with the previous project. This time, however, we'll make a little stronger "hatband" by double folding the bottom segment on this sideand tucking the top fold inside the "hatband."

Turn the project over. Then fold in the right and left side so they meet in the middle.

 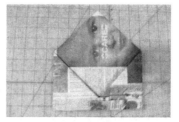

Turn up the outside corners so you can double fold the lower layer and tuck that into the "hatband."

At this point, you can fold the top of the triangle down, and then tuck that into the hatband as well, to make a flat-topped cap!

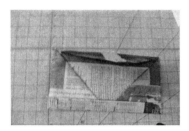 

As you can now see, there is a "pocket" formed where you can eventually put your head.

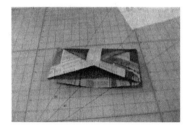

Now, we are going to open and smoosh the the pocket so the project is folded in the other direction.

Smooshing the project flat gives a **rhombus** (diamond shape). The corners of this diamond-shape can then be folded in and tucked into the headband.

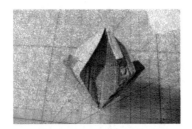 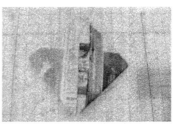

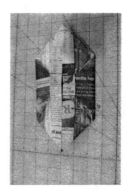

The resulting product can the be opened carefully and manipulated into an open box shape.

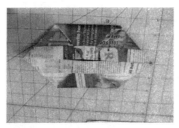 

Here are a few other views.

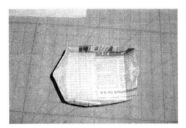 

"Capped off" with a demonstration of the product in use!

This will keep the paint and ink out of your hair, and when the job is done, simply throw it away and make another for future jobs!

Movie Cartoons from a Strip of Paper

Remember that strip of paper we trimmed off the letter-size sheet to make it square? Here's a use for it!

Fold the strip in half.

We are going to draw two pictures, one on each half that are slightly different to indicate something has moved.

Here, I've drawn a running stick person on the top sheet, and then the same stick figure in about the same position on the bottom sheet, with the arms and legs in different positions.

Then, I used my pencil to roll up the top sheet and put a curl in it so the top sheet tends to stay rolled up.

By rolling and unrolling the top sheet, just by moving the pencil. I see one of my drawings then the other.

If you do this fast enough, you can trick your eyes into thinking the figure is moving.

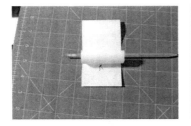 

You can probably think of a lot of possibilities for this, such as a running horse, or someone jumping.

You could even write secret messages by writing only parts of the letters on the top sheet and the remaining parts on the bottom. you could only read the message by tricking your eyes into seeing both parts at once.

I've also made more complex "motion cartoons by using a small pad of paper and making a number of pictures on several sheets. then you can flip through the pad to see the motion!

Secret Messages Written on Rubber Bands

Okay, so this one isn't made of paper, but I threw it in as a bonus, just because it's easy and kinda' neat!

Can't really read what's on this rubber band because the writing is all smooshed.

The way this was done was to stretch out the rubber band on a book or board, then write messages on it when it's stretched out.

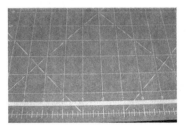

Relax the rubber band and it just looks like squiggles.

Stretch it out again, and your friend can read the message.

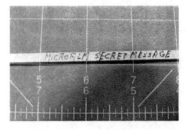

Might be fun to stick this into a valentine's Day card or a Birthday card without saying anything beforehand.

Think how your friend might puzzle over this briefly before figuring out how to "get the message!"

Maybe next time I update this book, I'll put in some more examples. What can you think of?

Dr. Bud Banis

banis@sciencehumanitiespress.com

CPSIA information can be obtained at www.ICGtesting.com
Printed in the USA
LVOW11s1847130714

394122LV00008B/299/P